The Journey of Discovery
Your Pathway to Purpose

A. L. Robinson

Young & One

Unless otherwise noted, all Scripture quotations are from the New Living Translation Version of the Bible. Used by permission.

First paperback edition January 2021.

Young & One products are available at special quantity discounts for bulk purchase for sales promotions, fundraising, and educational needs.

Book designs by Young & One Publishing
International Standard Book Number: 978-0-578-85248-5

Printed in the United States of America

Published by Young & One Publishing

www.weareyoungandone.com

Table of Contents

First and foremost, I want to thank my Heavenly Father for giving me this insight, as well as entrusting me to share this message with the world.

I want to acknowledge and thank my Good Thing, my wife, Mrs. Julisa Robinson. You've been more than encouraging and patient during this process. You are truly a gift, and I want to thank you for sticking by my side. You are the epitome of a helpmeet. Thank you for all that you do for our family. I love you, and I honor you.

Kylie & Amir, Daddy did it! I just want to make you guys proud – I love you two, and any others who may follow!

To my parents and grandparents, this is what it looks like when you sow a seed. Thank you, and I love you!

To my siblings, the rest of my family, and my friends, I love you all!

To any leaders who I have had the privilege of gleaning from, thank you for your guidance.

This book is dedicated to anyone who's still trying to figure life out, and find their "place." It is for you, the reader, who's simply trying to find the meaning of it all.

This book is also dedicated to all of the aspiring writers. Don't waste anymore time, write your way out.

You have purpose!

I know thy works: behold, I have set before thee an open door, and no man can shut it: for thou hast a little strength, and hast kept my word, and hast not denied my name.
-Revelation 3:8, KJV

INTRODUCTION

There was a young man who could land interviews with ease, and obtain his desired job the exact same day, simply because he had a contagious personality. Once he'd get hired on, however, his tenure would last no longer than a year. Things even reached a point to where all doors completely ceased opening for him.

Inevitability, he grew discouraged. He found himself upset with God, asking questions such as, "Why are you allowing this to happen to me?" and, "Do you not see all of my responsibilities?"

After a protracted period of time, he came to realize that God was actually trying to show him *himself*, as well as how he was viewed in His eyesight.

God wanted him to dig deeper, and to eventually discover that *thing*, that hidden treasure, which he already possessed within.

God knew the doors that the young man was chasing were no longer big enough to contain all that he possessed. In other words, his **purpose** was greater than any closed door.

Listen, I am that young man!

I have so much more to share with you, so let's get into it!

Let's start with a couple of definitions.

An entrepreneur is a person who operates a business, or several businesses, and takes on a major financial risk in order to do so.

Purpose is the reason for which something is done or created, or for which it exists.

When one discovers their purpose, and understands that there's a favorable merge waiting to take place as it relates to the vehicle of entrepreneurship, there is a latter experience of greatness that's fully ready to embrace him or her!

In other words, when you discover your purpose, it can lead to profit, thus enabling you to live life on your own terms!

One of the founding scriptures for my company, "The Visionaire Club," is Jeremiah 1:5, AMP. I leverage this scripture to help motivate others as it relates to stepping into their purpose. This is done in an effort to help them visualize how merging that treasure within, with entrepreneurship, can lead to wealth.

The main objective of my business, and for individuals who are drawn to my voice, is to ensure that they reach a place of **discovery**! In other words, I want to help you ensure that you discover what your God-given treasure is!!

In viewing Jeremiah 1:5, specifically the Amplified Version, it reads:

> *"Before I formed you in the womb, I knew you [and approved of you as My chosen instrument], and before you were born, I consecrated you [to Myself as My own]; I have appointed you as a prophet to the nations."*

There is so much substance in that one verse alone. Something in you should have immediately awaken to the idea that there is a need to further explore, as well as to discover, more than what you currently see!

Just in case that wasn't enough to get you digging deeper, allow me to assist you further. What I believe God is saying to us here is that before we were ever created, He gave us a unique identity. With that unique identity, He endorsed His elect for a tailored-made, or specific, purpose.

In the latter part of that scripture, He used the word *prophet*, in the context of saying "..appointed you as a prophet to the nations." The word prophet refers to a person who is observed as an inspired teacher, or proclaimer of the will of God.

So, as the appointed prophet when it comes to operating in your purpose, you have been given the authority to make an impact in your sphere of influence.

Two of the ways to discover your purpose, and/or what you are called to do, is through your experiences, as well as through your gifts/talents. Ultimately, in discovering your purpose, it creates a passion within that incites a life lived on your own terms.

In this book, I will help you to identify your purpose. Ultimately, you will develop a business idea. Keep in mind though, that this discovery is not simply for you to figure out how to monetize your gifting; rather, it is for you to have a real, genuine impact on the lives of those who you've been assigned to serve.

I want to be in agreement with you during this process. One of the ways that we can come into agreement is through the vehicle of prayer. I want you to pray this prayer, in faith, as you are on your journey of discovery!

Father God, first off, I just want to say thank You! Thank You for having me in mind as it relates to creation. You created me to do great exploits in this earth, through the vehicle of entrepreneurship, for Your name's sake. You created me to do great exploits, of which I can't even begin to imagine or fathom.

With my faith to journey forward, along with my will to discover the treasure that You've graced me with, I know that You will reveal Your purpose for me over the course of time. I understand that I must seek You for revelation as it pertains to Your will for my life.

*As I explore the following sections on experiences, as well as gifts/talents, I pray to find my hidden treasure within, the treasure called **purpose**.*

Now God, help me to get outside of myself, and to clear my mind of all doubts, fears, practical calculations, or anything that could hinder what I am seeking to accomplish throughout this process.

*I position my mind to receive **Kingdom**! I elevate to a realm where I am able to tap into, and grasp, your true intent for my life. Thank You for the ability to gather what I need in the spirit, and transfer it into the natural (my reality).*

I don't know when, or where, and I don't know the time, or the day, when I will reach that point of discovery, but I thank You in advance that there is a set time!

In the powerful name of Jesus I pray,

Amen!!

Remember, you were made in His image. So, while you don't have the supreme power to *be* God, you do have the power and authority to be *exactly* who He has called and predestined you to be. It's in His ability that you are able to become just that.

Listen, I'm excited for you! I'm excited for your journey of discovery, and I'm excited for how this ultimate discovery is going to make room for you to be that divine entrepreneur who you are destined to become.

I must give this disclaimer: this book is not intended to tell you <u>what</u> your purpose is. Truly, it's all about *your* JOURNEY OF DISCOVERY!!

In the next section, there's a questionnaire. I want you to take your time with this assessment, and answer all of the questions thoroughly.

I encourage you to go beyond the surface. I want you to really dig down deep when it comes to your answers. If you don't, you'll do yourself a major disservice as it relates to this journey; and we want a *reward*!

So, if you have to reflect and meditate on certain questions, do just that. This is your material, this is your life, and it is truly a journey.

The late great Nipsey Hussle said it best, "Instead of trying to build a brick wall, lay a brick every day. Eventually, you'll look up and you'll have a brick wall." That's the picture I'm trying to paint for you!

Don't try to discover your purpose in a single day.

If you make it your business to discover a little more each day, before you know it, your purpose will be fully unveiled, and you'll be operating in it in its totality.

Now, let's DIVE IN!

Ask, and it shall be given you; seek, and ye shall find; knock, and it shall be opened unto you:

-Matthew 7:7, KJV

QUESTIONNAIRE

1. Is there anything that you do with minimal effort?

_____

_____

_____

_____

_____

_____

_____

_____

_____

_____

_____

_____

_____

_____

_____

_____

_____

_____

_____

2. Do you have any skills? If so, what are those skills?

_____

_____

_____

_____

_____

_____

_____

_____

_____

_____

_____

_____

_____

_____

_____

_____

_____

_____

_____

_____

_____

3. What are you passionate about?

_____

_____

_____

_____

_____

_____

_____

_____

_____

_____

_____

_____

_____

_____

_____

_____

_____

_____

_____

_____

_____

4. What were you passionate about as a child?

_____

_____

_____

_____

_____

_____

_____

_____

_____

_____

_____

_____

_____

_____

_____

_____

_____

_____

_____

_____

_____

5. If money weren't an issue, and you could do anything with your time, what would you do with those 8 hours each day?

_____

_____

_____

_____

_____

_____

_____

_____

_____

_____

_____

_____

_____

_____

_____

_____

_____

_____

_____

_____

6. What do you get so lost in that you
   lose track of time?

_____

_____

_____

_____

_____

_____

_____

_____

_____

_____

_____

_____

_____

_____

_____

_____

_____

_____

_____

7. **If you could be remembered for 3 things after you die, what would they be?** *i.e., books, etc.; something that indicates you left your mark here.*

_____

_____

_____

_____

_____

_____

_____

_____

_____

_____

_____

_____

_____

_____

_____

_____

_____

_____

_____

_____

8. Whether as a child, or as an adult, was there anything that you wanted to do, but you were <u>discouraged</u> from doing it?

_____

_____

_____

_____

_____

_____

_____

_____

_____

_____

_____

_____

_____

_____

_____

_____

_____

_____

9. Assess yourself: Does what you currently make an hour equate to your worth? What is an hour of your time worth?

_____

_____

_____

_____

_____

_____

_____

_____

_____

_____

_____

_____

_____

_____

_____

_____

_____

_____

_____

10. Have you endured anything in life that you overcame, which you can now help someone else overcome?

_____

_____

_____

_____

_____

_____

_____

_____

_____

_____

_____

_____

_____

_____

_____

_____

_____

_____

_____

_____

_____

11. If your family had a mandatory project due, what would they be confident in choosing your role to be?

_____

_____

_____

_____

_____

_____

_____

_____

_____

_____

_____

_____

_____

_____

_____

_____

_____

_____

_____

12. When people seek you out for advice, what is it usually in regards too?

_____

_____

_____

_____

_____

_____

_____

_____

_____

_____

_____

_____

_____

_____

_____

_____

_____

_____

_____

13. Describe yourself in one word?

14. PERSPECTIVE: How do you determine success?: Is it by a set dollar amount and misery, or by uncertainty and happiness?

_____

_____

_____

_____

_____

_____

_____

_____

_____

_____

_____

_____

_____

_____

_____

_____

_____

_____

_____

_____

15. If your job were to let you go tomorrow, how would you survive?

_____

_____

_____

_____

_____

_____

_____

_____

_____

_____

_____

_____

_____

_____

_____

_____

_____

_____

_____

_____

16. Does anything bother you, to the extent that you think/say, "Someone needs to fix this!"?

_____

_____

_____

_____

_____

_____

_____

_____

_____

_____

_____

_____

_____

_____

_____

_____

_____

_____

_____

17. What isn't working for you? What drains you, causes you to feel stressed, or wastes your time?

_____

_____

_____

_____

_____

_____

_____

_____

_____

_____

_____

_____

_____

_____

_____

_____

_____

_____

_____

_____

_____

_____

Now that you've taken the questionnaire, my prayer is that you have a better understanding of yourself.

Hopefully, you were able to recollect a few things, and possibly reconnected with some of your childhood memories, and/or desires.

Throughout the duration of this process, I want you to view what you have written down/discovered as your building blocks, and use them accordingly as you continue to journey towards discovering your purpose.

What you've written down are your context clues.

As you dig deeper, you will begin to rediscover things that you may have buried years ago.

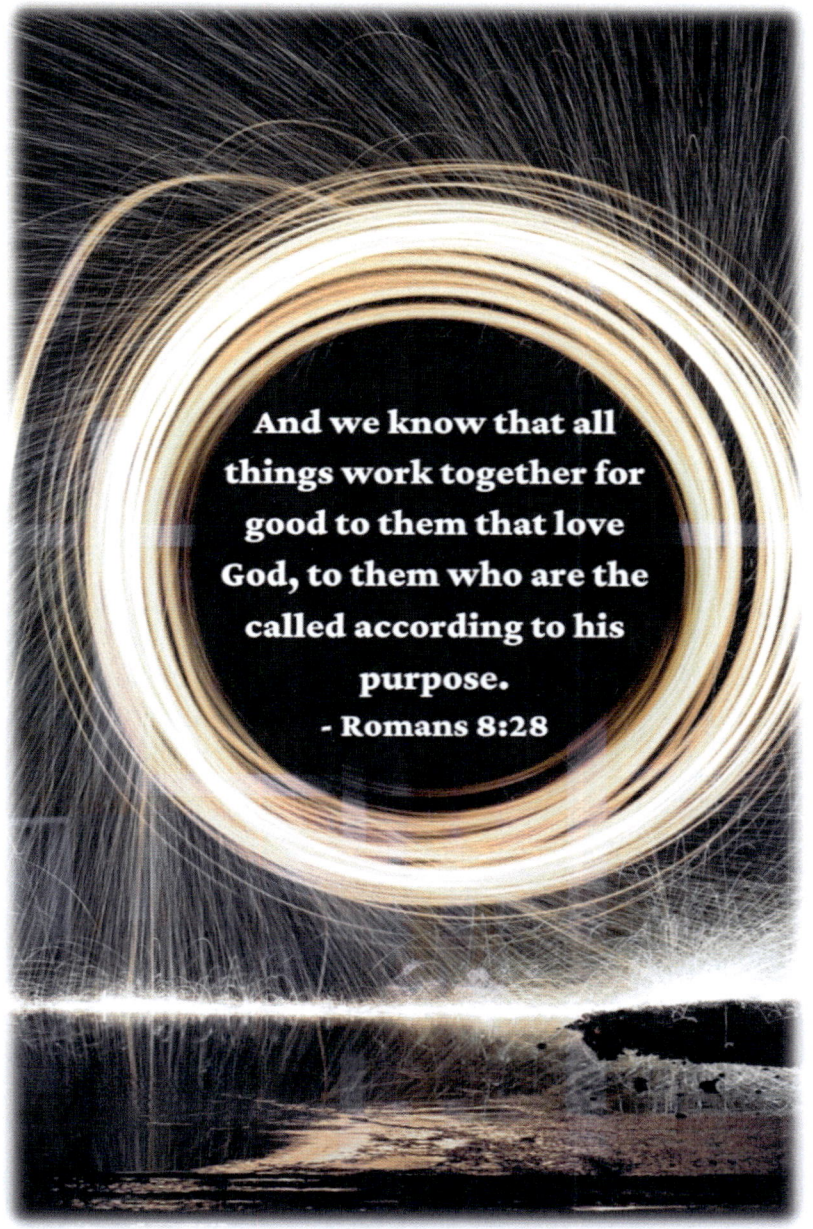

And we know that all things work together for good to them that love God, to them who are the called according to his purpose.
- Romans 8:28

THE IMPORTANCE OF VISION & EXPERIENCE

In the Bible (*Genesis, Chapters: 37-50*), Joseph was what we would consider to be, "the chosen one." He was the one who was called out of his family to do something great. The fact that he was chosen wasn't readily received by his brothers. This was mainly due to the fact that what Joseph was operating in, simply wasn't the norm.

Due to the fact that Joseph wasn't received by his brothers, I believe this caused him to have a hard time accepting himself as well; just the isolation and being misunderstood, which are often byproducts of being "the chosen one."

This example alone points to the fact that we often can't conceive the vastness of our purpose, typically because it has never been done before in our bloodline!

We've been programmed to think one thing, but even Jesus came to break tradition.

Tradition, in this instance, could be your job! Working for someone else has probably been your family's custom, and God is trying to get you to step out and be the tradition-breaker.

He's trying to make you the example. The one who sets the tone to where stepping into ownership becomes the new norm for your bloodline.

Listen, you're reading this book right now because **YOU ARE THE ONE**!

You are the one who knows that you simply cannot do life as NORMAL. You don't have a blueprint, because it's outside of the norm.

God gave Joseph a glimpse. He gave him a dream that he would be made ruler over his brothers, which eventually caused them to despise him. When God reveals something to us, we often forget that there's a process involved in order to obtain what He has spoken.

Let me insert that at the beginning of this section, I posted the scriptures where you can read Joseph's account in the Bible. If you aren't familiar with this story, or if you just want to go back and read it again, you have that point of reference so that you are able to do so.

Once Joseph survived the pit that he was thrown into by his brothers, they ended up selling him into captivity. He was sold to the Ishmaelites for twenty shekels of silver. Subsequent to such, the Ishmaelites turned around and sold Joseph into slavery, where he landed in the hands of the Egyptians.

Hopefully you're following along with me; I'm going to help us make the connection here in just a moment.
The glimpse that God had given Joseph, caused jealousy to brew amongst his brothers, which ultimately led to his **EXPERIENCE**.

While in captivity as a slave, Joseph showed himself faithful. He was diligent as it related to working in the palace. This was his experience at that particular time in his life. This is often the *place* where purpose tends to get lost. This is the point in your life where nothing seems to line up with the vision, or glimpse, that God previously gave you.

While working in the palace, Potiphar's wife attempted to make sexual advances at Joseph, but Joseph refused. Although he refused, she still ended up falsely accusing him of attempting to rape her. Ultimately, this landed him in prison.

At this juncture in his life, I probably would've asked myself, "How is my life adding up to the vision/glimpse that You gave me, God?" It's important to note, however, that through everything that transpired in Joseph's life, it was all adding to his overall experience.

Around the latter part of his time in prison, Joseph was accompanied by two other prisoners: a cupbearer and a chief baker. It is important to note that they both ended up having a dream. After sharing their dreams with Joseph, He was able to accurately interpret them both.

The cupbearer received a favorable interpretation of his dream. In that moment, Joseph asked that he would remember him in the presence of Pharaoh.

When the chief baker saw that Joseph had given the cupbearer a favorable interpretation, he shared his dream with him in order to receive interpretation as well; on the contrary though, it was interpreted that he would die.

Shortly thereafter, it was Pharaoh's birthday. Just as Joseph had interpreted, he restored the cupbearer to his position, but the chief baker was executed!

At this juncture, a couple of years had passed by since the cupbearer was released from prison. Joseph was still in prison, seemingly *forgotten*.

I want you to stop reading for a second, and say to yourself, "**I am not forgotten! There is an appointed time set for me**!" I want you to say it until you believe it!

Now, let's continue!

One day, the Egyptian ruler, Pharaoh, had a dream. His dream was so pressing that it was causing him to lose sleep. In other words, the dream was troubling Pharaoh. It troubled him so much, that he sent for all of the men of Egypt who were trained to interpret dreams, to come before him and interpret his dream.

Now, I know it's not "proper biblical or religious etiquette" to say this, but as the expression goes, he simply had no luck.

All awhile though, there was a key person in the midst of this situation who witnessed the constant failures of those who couldn't properly interpret Pharaoh's dream: **the cupbearer**.

It's as if the lightbulb went off in his head, and he *remembered* Joseph! The cupbearer ended up sharing with Pharaoh that there was a man in prison who accurately interpreted His dream.

Pharaoh sent guards to the prison to go and retrieve Joseph, all in the hopes that he could help interpret his dream.

Well, Joseph did just that! He was able to interpret Pharaoh's dream, and because of that, Joseph found favor in Pharaoh's sight.

In fact, Joseph was granted supreme authority over all of the Egyptians, as a non-Egyptian, simply because he had the ability to interpret dreams.

Now, just to give you a quick synopsis, Joseph interpreted that God was warning Pharaoh that there would be a famine in the land. Armed with this information, Joseph came up with a strategy so that the people could be preserved for the duration of the famine.

Not only was Egypt set to be affected by this famine, but the surrounding areas were as well. This included Canaan, which was where Joseph's family resided. Simply put, he was going to be positioned to save his family, including his brothers, who had once betrayed him.

This is why you must guard your heart. When you're being processed, or going through an experience, the enemy will always highlight the negative. This is done in an attempt to keep your eyes off of the promise.

If you don't guard your heart, you may begin to agree with the negative thoughts, which can push you further away from purpose. If Joseph had allowed what he experienced to outweigh the promise, he never would've been in position to fulfill his purpose.

This is why it is so imperative for us to have a real relationship with God. We must be mature enough to know that the God we serve is very strategic. So strategic, in fact, that everything He does and allows in our lives, is tailor-made to ensure that we fulfill our purpose.

The scripture that I'm about to share with you is going to absolutely blow your mind. In this text, Joseph is talking to his brothers who once betrayed him. I have to share it out of the Good News Translation, well, because this is truly **good news**!

Joseph said to his brothers, *"God sent me ahead of you, to rescue you in this amazing way, and to make sure that you and your descendants survive. So, it was not really you who sent me here, but God. He has made me the king's highest official. I am in charge of his whole country; I am the ruler of all Egypt."*
- Genesis 45:7-8, Good News Translation

Wow! That's it! I hope it's becoming as lucid to you as crystal clear water, that the glimpse which Joseph had, was actually filtering itself through his experience, that he might ultimately discover his purpose.

In other words, the betrayal was necessary, the lies were necessary, the imprisonment was necessary, because it catapulted him to fulfill the vision that God had given him years prior.

Joseph's story is recounted in the Book of Genesis, but we can see how a scripture found later in the Bible, *Romans 8:28*, suddenly comes alive through his life's journey.

In short, we can see how everything that Joseph had to walk through, actually ended up working together for his good.

When God gives us a "glimpse," he doesn't provide us with all of the details regarding how we'll reach that ultimate destination. Instead, He allows us to journey through our experiences, and in turn, the purpose behind it all is revealed over the course of time.

Joseph's ultimate purpose was once a glimpse, but because he endured hardness as a good soldier, everything that God promised him, became his reality.

I want to encourage you as it pertains to your life. There are some distinct promises that God has given you, but they wouldn't have the potential to come into fruition lest you had experienced what you've experienced.

In short, **it was all necessary**!

I'm not sure if this part has taken you back to an experience as a child, as teenager, or even as an adult, but it was all necessary!

We may find ourselves in situations where things are difficult and challenging, but these things literally occur because God has a plan concerning our lives.

I'm sure it hurt in the moment, and it probably even caused you to lose some sleep. There's no doubt, it cost you a lot along the way, but without that pain, and without that trial, there was no way that you could have gotten to your promise, which is the fulfillment of your purpose.

Some of you may still be in a situation right now that's causing you a lot of pain, but I want to encourage you by saying **don't stop, press through the pain, and you will discover your purpose**.

Declare this out of your mouth, "The devil can no longer play me as a victim, so he better respect me as a victor!"

One of the things I've learned throughout life is to not get so caught up in the problem, that you fail to find the solution. A solution is always going to be wrapped up in a problem.

I pray that Joseph's account was the perfect example for you. It's very possible that this was the section of the book that you needed to aid you as you are on your journey to discovering purpose.

I'm going to conclude this section with this: Joseph's purpose was bigger than him. An entire nation was dependent upon him discovering his purpose. So let me ask you, who might be depending on you to discover yours?

I say to you, walk in your purpose!

If you want to dissect this section until you're able to relate it to you own life, start with these questions. *only if there's a need and it's applicable.

1. What was your glimpse?

2. What is the problem that your solution is currently (or was) wrapped up in?

A man's gift maketh room for him, and bringeth him before great men.
- Proverbs 18:16, KJV

GIFTS/TALENTS

Now, I want to talk to my gifted/talented people. You know you're gifted, you can easily identify it, but you're sitting on your gift.

You may have the gift to read music, the gift to motivate others, the gift to coach, etc. If that's you, I have to let you know that when you're gifted, *others benefit* from your gift. So, why not turn your gift into a business?

How many people need a coach? Can you motivate others when they lose their momentum? How many people are complaining about their lack of food options? Can you cook?

What's stopping you from sharing that Heaven-sent recipe, or that remarkable, great tasting, food truck selection?

What's your gift?

My wife is gifted at editing and revising, so naturally, she's a publisher. It would be a rhetorical question if you asked me whether or not she edited and published this book for me. You already know she did, with her gifted self!

Some of you are probably Lebron James fans. That dude is a GOAT! Look at Lebron's success. Now, I'm not neglecting the fact that he has worked hard, because he has an unbelievable work ethic. At the time of this publication, he's currently in his 18th year in the NBA, and still looks younger and more finessed than some of the new and upcoming players; but news flash, Lebron was BORN to do this!

In other words, it doesn't take much for him to operate in his *gift*. His presence is a gift.

You could, in fact, put Lebron on the worst team in the NBA today, and that same team will immediately become contenders!

When you have a gift, you have to hone in on it and perfect it.

I hope I'm causing someone's spirit to leap right now. I pray that you're able to readily identify your gift, and are now sensing how the world is waiting for your arrival.

There is a GRACE when you flow in your gift.

I'm attempting to help you see the true value that your gift holds. Your gift(s) will indeed make room for you, and bring you before great men.

I can't stop using Bron Bron as a center piece in this section, because it's illuminating the fact that everything you need in order to live your abundant, purposeful life, is already at your disposal.

If Lebron didn't choose to be great by flowing in his gift, then the vision for other areas in which he now partakes in would have never been birthed.

There would be no iPromise School, no lifetime Nike endorsement, no partnership with the University of Akron to provide scholarships for underprivileged children, none of that would exist.

Now, to my talented people, what skill have you learned, that you now have the aptitude to teach to others?

A talent is a skill that's learned, a gift is a natural ability, but they both have value, and they both serve a purpose.

Maybe you've learned the art of public speaking. Could it be possible that the person who gets overly anxious when he or she has to speak before a crowd, may need a service to overcome that fear?

Or, maybe you are a persuasive individual who knows how to sell and market really well. I'm sure that up and coming business, or the business that's on the verge of going under, could utilize your expertise.

It's all about purpose!

When it comes to a talent, or a skill, there's so much that falls under this category.

I can almost guarantee that from the list I have attached below, something will register in your spirit (even if it's not on this list).

Public Speaking
Writing
Art
Photography
Money Management
Typing
Strategic Planning
Raising Money
Sales
Logistics
Risk Management
Singing
Research
Advertising
Taxes
Teaching
Credit Repair
Financial Planning

And the list goes on!

Some of you may be called to ministry. You've truly been marked with a gift as it pertains to ministry. The gifts are as follows:

Administration
Apostleship/Pioneering
Discernment
Exhortation
Evangelism
Faith
Forgiving
Hospitality
Knowledge
Leadership
Pastor/Shepherd
Prophecy
Teacher
Serving
Showing mercy
Wisdom

When it comes to the aforementioned offices, you are probably already operating in your gift, outside of the church, without a title. So, once you accept the call, there will be a definite grace upon you once you operate in your gift within the church.

When your Spirit knows that there's more, but you don't take the initiative to tap into what your Spirit already knows, you begin to grieve your Spirit.

One of my prayer points is that my Spirit will always be in communion with the Father.

I want you to adopt that prayer point, because the Spirit that resides on the inside of you has insight as it relates to the plans that the Father has for your life.

Listen, don't forsake your Helper on this journey of discovery.

It's as if, in fact, you're doing life with a personal assistant.

I love talking to people about their gifts and talents.

I've come to find that it's not so much that individuals don't know that they're gifted and talented, but where the issue arises, however, is in them not feeling adequate enough to fully operate in that gift or talent.

When you come to grips with the fact that it's not in your ability, but rather God's ability *through* you to operate in that gift/ talent, it dispels the very thought of not being *enough*.

I stand on the belief that if you develop a genuine relationship with God, you will begin to know you, the REAL you, and thus flow in your purpose.

Deuteronomy 8:18 (KJV) says:

"But thou shalt remember the Lord thy God: for it is He that giveth thee power to get wealth, that He may establish His covenant which He sware unto thy fathers, as it is this day."

God's word says that He has given us the ability to obtain wealth.

Simply put, it's time to tap in!

God has given you the key to your prosperity!

It's one thing to *discover* your purpose, but it's another thing to **operate** in it.

Your provision is released when you're in the flow of your purpose.

God forbid, especially as you are journeying towards discovering your purpose, but if you were to lose your job, or even if you are unemployed right now, God, the Source, has embedded *something* in you (gift/talent) that will cause you to succeed, no matter what you may face.

For this reason, you do not have to experience lack.

Declarations are key.

When you declare a thing, you're literally surging power into those words by speaking what you want to see!

So, let's declare a thing!

*"God, You placed a gift/talent within me! You placed it within me to live out my purpose, as well as to obtain wealth! Wealth that surpasses me, **generational wealth**!*

Help me to discover that gift, if I haven't already. If I have, I acknowledge You, from this point on, as the One who invested it in me.

I will not bury my gift, but instead, I give it to You as a return on Your investment! I choose to allow You to have Your way with these gifts/talents that You have placed on the inside of me.

In Your ability, and not my own, I will see the true value in what You've entrusted me with! Purpose will be fulfilled, and impact will be made, for Your Kingdom!"

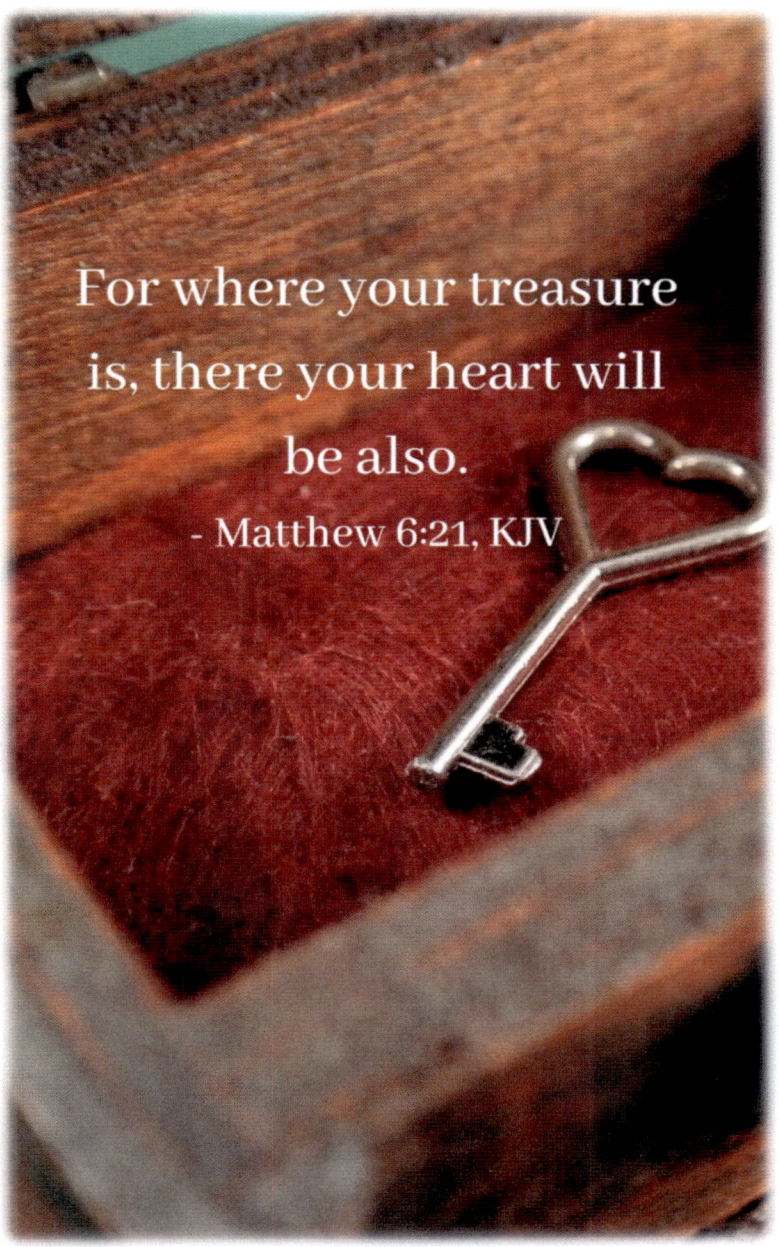

For where your treasure is, there your heart will be also.

- Matthew 6:21, KJV

PASSION

At this point in your journey, my prayer is that you've either discovered, or are at least a step closer to discovering, your purpose.

It is when one discovers their purpose, that it turns into passion!

Passion is a strong, and barely controllable emotion.

When purpose becomes your passion, it derives from the heart.

In other words, it flows from you so effortlessly, that you're willing to do it for free.

Even when you turn it into a business, it doesn't feel laborious.

At this juncture, I want you to let out a sigh of relief.

You've been journeying, and now you've discovered why you are currently walking this earth, Champ! I call you Champ, because you're a champion!

From this point forward, all you're going to do is win!

You now see why life is worth *living*. All those years of you questioning yourself, doubting yourself, feeling worthless – for some of you all, although you've been financially stable, you've still felt **unfulfilled** – you can officially divorce those negative thoughts!

Those false feelings, and those dark days, are over!

As I sit here, all that I can think about is the overwhelming joy that you're feeling right now, and how I felt when I first discovered my purpose.

The imagery was so clear.

I literally saw myself as a child, wrapped up in the arms of our Heavenly Father. It was as if He was affirming the little boy in me, to become the man who I was always predestined to become.

I couldn't help but cry that day, but those were tears of joy!

Although it took some time to fully materialize, I saw a glimpse that day.

So, whether you have a full understanding of your purpose, or if you only have a glimmer of what shall be, I want to encourage you by saying that your steps are indeed ordered by God!

I'm cheering you on as you continue your

journey of discovery!

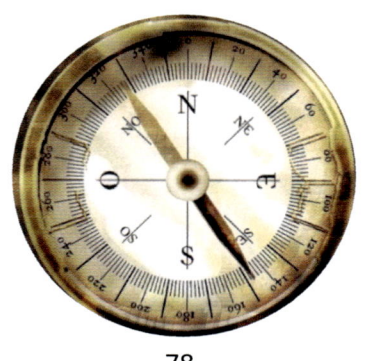

To Contact A.L. Robinson

Email: ceovisionaireclub@gmail.com

www.weareyoungandone.com

Additional Notes

Made in the USA
Columbia, SC
23 March 2021